Spirituality And Symmetry

Shiva & Shakti, and the balance between the Two

Kunal Goswami

BookLeaf Publishing

India | USA | UK

Made with ❤ on the BookLeaf Publishing Platform

www.bookleafpub.in

www.bookleafpub.com

Dedication

*To my Soul city **Rishikesh** and **Dev Bhumi Uttarakhand**, where my soul finds peace.*

Preface

I write. Now whether it can be considered as poems or not, I leave it up to you.

Spirituality and Symmetry is a reflection of my personal path—one that led me to profound realizations about Shiva and Shakti, the eternal dance of masculine and feminine energies, and the balance that exists within us all.

In this book of short poetries, I have written poems about my experiences, the theories and concepts which I have learnt on my way; and also poems about some of the best people who have been absolutely kind to me.

It is about embracing both stillness and movement, solitude and connection, acceptance and surrender.

With love and gratitude,
Kunal

Acknowledgements

My Mummy, for bringing me into existence.
Ganga Maa, for accepting me as your child.
Muskaan, for existing. You're the Best!
Anu Vijoy, my brother from another mother.
Ann-Christin Sophie Berardi, my favourite European Lady.
Pavithra K, for being absolutely true to yourself.

Last but not the least -
Monika ji, Suraj ji, Shruti Akka, Shakuntala Naik, Olga, Cari, Rushi and Andrea —thank you for being part of my journey.

With love and gratitude, this book is for you.

1. Ardhnarishwar

As a kid growing up, I used to visit my maternal
grandparents' home during vacations.
They had a portrait of Ardhnarishwar hung on the wall
in one of the rooms.
Half Man, Half Woman.
As I grew up, I learnt it was Shiva and Shakti in the form
of Ardhnarishwar.

Years later, when I went to Rishikesh,
I learnt in the teachings of Yoga that everyone on this
planet have a feminine and masculine side;
irrespective of gender.
The feminine side on the half left and masculine on the
half right of the body.

Our face is not symmetric.
If you take a photograph of your face; crop it vertically
from the middle, you get two halves.
Reverse the orientation of both halves, join the left with
mirrored left and right with mirrored right.
You will see two different people.

There is an Asymmetry.
There is a distinct left and right.

Shiva & Shakti.
Moon & Sun.
Ha & Tha.

For some,
the energy leans more towards the left;
for some, it is towards the right.
Those who have their energy centered right between
feminine and masculine,
are called Yogis.

2. Shiva and Shakti

I find it beautiful; yet weirdly incomplete,
that we pray to; and think of Shiva as a separate entity.

Shiva, the highest source of energy!,
He, who holds the power to destroy a Universe in a
blink,
is incomplete without Shakti
He, Mahadev!
is vulnerable, if not for HER

However; there's a difference,
between being vulnerable and being weak

When vulnerable;
You open yourself,
to connections..
to love..
to life..

Vulnerability leads to creation,
Weakness to destruction..

Vulnerability leads to becoming strong!
Soul and Positivity :)

3. Spirituality

Every game has different rules..

Different sections of life;
Suppress You, Depress you

Red light, you stop..
Green light, you go..

You are a kid, get good marks in school, fulfill your
parent's expectations
You are an adult, keep your emotions in check
You are a girl, follow the rules of patriarchy
You are a boy, act tough

What do I do if I want to let it all out?
What if I want to shout and scream?
What if I want to break free?

Spirituality - Come here kid.
We got no rules.
Laugh. Cry. Scream. Shout.
Dance in the rain.
Jump in the lake.
No judgements.

Just the kindness and compassion to all beings. Love and
positivity :)

4. Symmetry

Left and Right,
Feminine and Masculine;
Consciousness lies somewhere between
Life and Death

Learning and Teaching,
Asking for help and Helping..

Clockwise and Anticlockwise,
The circle completes

The soul evolves
and merges with universe,
when one realizes
the Shiva and Shakti within..
and the symmetry between the two

5. Divine Femininity

There's an energy,
Feminine in nature.
It comes to protect you,
when you need it the most.

This energy,
is fierce and overwhelming,
yet maternal.
This energy,
binds the Earth together.

This energy; comes to you in form of humans,
and the elements of mother nature.
She comes to you in form of a gentle butterfly,
or a roaring river.

She guides you,
if you choose to listen to her carefully.
Just bow your head and accept her blessing.

The aspect of Divine femininity,
if and when awakened,
protects you, and change your destiny.

6. Home

When someone asks me,
Where are you from?
I answer "a lot of places"

People usually laugh at the answer,
I laugh with them too..
The joke is on them :D

Everywhere I go
Mostly Villages and towns, and some cities
They have their own charm,
And a unique differentiative energy..
A particular pace;
between the land and the residing people

When you connect with the soul of a land,
She gives you a part of her soul
And keeps a part of your soul within herself
This connection is eternal
Forever etched in the soul of the land :)

This is why,
Some places feel strangely familiar
Some land feels home..

Because in another life;
Some previous incarnation,
You inhabited there

The land remembers your soul
You're home :)

7. Rishikesh

My whole Life, I have always felt like an outsider,
Never found a place where I belonged..
Roamed around everywhere,
To find something that was always evasive.

I had given up.
Until some time ago,
I went to a town.
It was filled with healers.
More healers come to this town from all over the world.
It was magic.

The saints and the sages,
meditated on this land
for thousand of years..
where nature flows in the forests,
and the river who is a mother,
Maa Ganga

I belonged here. I found home. I was home.

8. Soul Group

have you ever met someone
who reminded you of another person
similar vibe
yet profoundly different energy

same kindness
same positivity

sometimes I wonder
are such people
part of a same soul?

A soul, which divided into multiples
and each part grew
on a different path
in a different direction
in a different galaxy
or a different universe whole together

9. Inner Peace

Ever seen a storm?
From the inside?

It's the most peaceful thing to experience.

That's where,
You do nothing.
You are nothing.
Absolutely thoughtless.

In the overwhelming chaos;
and the brutal whirlpools,
You learn to see the beauty of everything,
that encompasses you around.

What do you do then?
Nothing.
You Surrender.
That's when you merge,
with the Universe.
That's when,
You see the MAGIC unfold.

10. Happy Mother's Day - 8th May, 2022

I went to Shivpuri today.

There's a white sand beach along which Maa Ganga flows.

The surroundings were surreal.
Practiced Yoga for about an hour.
Felt exhilarating.

There was a storm of emotions inside me.
I went to the bank of river and dipped my feet inside.

Then I screamed;
I shouted.
As loud as I could.

I felt overwhelmed.
Then I cried.

A lot of things blocking my energy cleared.
I trust fell face down into the water,
and it felt like Maa Ganga took me into her embrace.

11. Surrender / Rebirth

Context: While river rafting in Rishikesh, I fell into water during the third rapid - golf course. After the initial few seconds where I was scared, I surrendered. I let the flow of river take me where she wanted to. I went into whirlpool twice and came back to surface, and floated with the flow. Initially scared, but never once afraid.

To evolve,
You must die
and be born again

Let yourself go
into the embrace of mother nature

She knows,
You are her child

That day
an element of mother nature
Water
asked me to surrender
and I did

I died
Maa Ganga took me in her embrace
and revived me

It was, as if
I was born a new
She gave birth to me
from her own womb :)

12. Araṇyānī (अरण्यानि)

Her soul is already evolved,
Vibrating at a much higher frequency.

She connects with the elements of the Universe,
comes and goes as she please..

I have seen her, in her zone,
Shining Blue Butterflies surrounds her in concentric
circles,
building up her Aura,
like the shining lights of Aurora..

She speaks with animals—and they reply,
Drawn to her as stars to sky.
They gather near, in quiet grace,
As if her presence sanctifies the space.

She feels what most can never name,
The pulse beneath the forest flame.
Nature bends to her soft tone—
As if her soul and roots are one.

She's psychic, intuitive,
harnesses the energy of Nature,

as if, it's an extension to her..

She bears the power soft yet wild,
The Goddess roams in her, beguiled.
With eyes that see what lies between,
Protective. Strong. Serene.

In folklores, she walks unseen—
The forest's heart, the mystic queen.

Fearless, wise, forever free...
with an Awakened Kundalini,
in Hinduism,
She is called Araṇyānī (अरण्यानि)

13. Metaphors

I like to speak in metaphors..
I don't want everyone to understand me.
only those,
who try to understand
what I am trying to convey.

My inner child;
lacked emotional connections,
while growing up.

maybe that's why,
I try to indulge
in deep conversations.

not many understand,
and that's ok.

cause when it's loud,
everyone notices..
when it's subtle,
not everyone has
the eyes to follow..

14. Perception

The thing about the perception is -
It changes.

You are going through a journey,
through a Transformation..
And let me tell you my friend,
The phases of any Transformation can be messy..
A butterfly seems beautiful, but the larva looks ugly..

Always REMEMBER the people,
who were there with you,
in the ugly weird phase..
Those who cared enough,
to bypass the creepy exterior,
And looked inside your soul..
Those who cared to LISTEN,
to the troubled inner child..

Once the cover of the book changes,
Everyone wants to read it..
Those are the best,
Who don't judge a book by it's cover..

Because; that's the thing about Perception -
It changes.

15. Kedarnath and Bhimshila

It was Almost about 4 in the morning.
Brahm Muhurt.
I was standing in the Queue.

In front of me, was Kedarnath temple.
The snowy mountains, in the background, they glowed.
I was soaking it all in, all the blessings,
My hands and feet bare.

The energy of the mountains,
I felt them blessing me.
I bowed my head, liberated.
I couldn't contemplate,
what to do with this positive flow of energy.

When the temples gates opened,
I went in and prayed.

After that, I went to **Bhimshila**—
The sacred rock that saved the temple from the flood.
I placed both my hands on it.
Suddenly, I felt a **rush—like water surging through me.**
It was intense.

I pulled my hands back.
It felt like the rock remembered
What it had faced.
And it showed it to me.

Slowly, I placed my hands again.
This time, I stayed.
I became one with it.
I let the memory of that water
Flow through me.
It was pure...
A blessing beyond words.

And when you receive such a blessing...
What can you do?

मैं नतमस्तक रह गया।

16. Guardian Angels

Has it ever happened to you?
You step out of your door,
Walk to your motorcycle—or maybe your car—
And mutter, *"Damn... I forgot the key."*
You head back in, grab it,
And somehow, ten minutes slip by.

It's rare, isn't it?
You usually follow a rhythm—
Keys in the same spot,
Routine like clockwork.

The future hold infinite possibilities.
We do not know what the future holds.
But, there is an entity which protects us,
that entity is a Guardian Angel.

A Guardian Angel is a higher power; always looking out
for you,
and knows all the variables and possibilities of the
future.

If you had left at exact time as you do everyday,
one possibility was - you might have met a life

threatening accident,
at a particular spot at a specific time to the dot second.

But, the Guardian angel makes you forget the key,
You were delayed.
You never reached that intersection.
You were saved.

Next time you forget your key,
Thank your Guardian angel.

17. Hanuman Dada

In Gujarati, "Dada" means grandfather—
But metaphorically, it can also mean a wise, protective soul.

And among all,
Hanuman Dada is the wisest.
The strongest.

The *Hanuman Chalisa* is no ordinary prayer—
It's a powerful stotra (hymn),
A shield for those who chant it with a pure intent.

I remember—
I was in 11th standard.
I had just learned to ride a scooter,
And like most teenagers,
I rode fast, a bit too fast.

One day, while speeding through a cross-section,
I lost control and slipped.
The right side of my head was about to hit a divider—
Hard.

But in that split second,

I felt something.
A hand.
Right beneath my forehead.

And I heard a voice—
Calm, powerful:
"I'm saving you this time...
But never drive hastily again."

I blacked out for a few minutes.
But when I woke up,
I was completely fine.
Not a single scratch.

It could have been serious.
Fatal, even.
But Hanuman Dada protected me.

From that day on,
I rode with care.
I've had a few minor accidents since then—
But nothing serious.
Because I was mindful.

And I knew—
He has always been watching over me.

18. Sikhism and the start of My Spiritual journey

ना कोई सवाल, ना कोई जवाब,
सिर्फ नूर, मेरे सिर उत्ते चमकदा।
बैठ गया, साँस लिया, अखां मुँद गइयां,
अते रूह उड्डी—आज़ाद, रोशन, नवीं।

It was in 2011,
I went to Pushkar with two of my friends,
one of them - Kanwaljeet Singh, who introduced me to
Sikhism.

There is Gurudwara Sahib,
just at the entrance of Pushkar city.

It was my first time visiting a Gurudwara (Sikh temple).
In Gurudwaras, there is a small pool of water, where you
wash your feet before entering.

I washed my feet,
and as soon as I put my first step inside,
I felt peace. For the first time in my life.
It was magic. Surreal.
I felt a higher energy blessed me in that moment.

I bowed down in front of Guru Granth Sahib,
Sat in the prayer hall and meditated,
the first time I experienced Spirituality.

No questions asked, no answers expected.
A pure form of energy, blessed me for life.
My Soul transcended - to freedom, to light.

19. My First Solo Trip: The Dream and the Journey

In April 2011,
I saw a dream.
There was a lake.
I was sitting by the edge, next to a wise old saint.
He had kind eyes, a soft white beard, and a white scarf tied over his head—much like a turban.
We weren't speaking at first. We were playing—splashing the still water with small rocks, laughing like children.
Then he looked at me, smiled gently, and said, "Come, son."

When I woke up, I didn't fully understand what I had seen. But something inside me knew:
That was Guru Nanak Dev Ji.

That year, during Diwali, I made a decision.
I travelled from Udaipur to Amritsar.

Alone.
And yet, not alone.
All along the way, I felt a subtle but powerful presence—a guarding energy around me. Like invisible hands

guiding me gently forward.

I met many Sikh people during that journey. Strangers,
yet somehow familiar.
They were kind. Warm. Full of light.
When they heard I was going to Amritsar for Diwali,
they smiled and said I was blessed.
Maybe they saw something I hadn't yet fully realized.

When I finally reached Harmandir Sahib, I felt
something shift in me.
I stayed there.
Slept beside the holy lake, under the stars.
Ate in the Langar with people from every corner of life—
no caste, no class, just humanity.
I prayed. I sat in silence.

I watched the light reflect off the water.
And I felt... peace.

Not just comfort, not just happiness—
But real, grounded, soul-deep peace.

That night, in the glow of Diwali lamps, surrounded by
devotion and stillness,
I accepted Sikhism—not as a label, but as a way of living.

20. The Gate

*Context: Something which I experienced through my
own spirit. What I saw and felt... it wasn't just a vision;
it was a journey between veils.*

In Ujjain, just outside the gates of Kaalbhairav Mandir,
I took off my shoes and placed them in the designated
spot.

Barefoot, I turned toward the temple—
And that's when it happened.
I looked up at the face of Kaalbhairav carved atop the
gate,
and in an instant, I went into trance.

What I saw next was beyond time and thought:
A vision of a Goddess, gentle and kind,
clothed entirely in white, standing above the clouds.
She was the Goddess of Life.
Without speaking, she reached out and held my hand.

She led me toward a Gate—one that divided two worlds.
On the other side, I saw clouds made of fiery red flames,
swirling and alive.
From within the gate, another figure appeared.

The contrast was stark.
The second Goddess—fierce, intense, her body covered in
black paint,
eyes wide, hair wild,
yet something about her felt unmistakably familiar.
There was a terrifying grace in her form—raw and
primal.
She was the Goddess of Death.

And then I knew—
She was my Kuldevi. Kali Maa.

The Goddess of Life gently passed me over to her.

Kali Maa held my hand, never letting go, and took me
into her realm.

What I witnessed was chaos—
a Queendom of fire and fury.
The sky roared, the clouds burned.
I walked barefoot over lava and flame,
yet my feet felt nothing.

I saw tormented souls, heard cries that pierced through
worlds,
Everyone in some sort of Loop.

and still, I felt no fear.
Because She was with me.

When the time came,
Kali Maa brought me back to the Gate,
where the Goddess of Life was waiting with a smile.

She placed my hand back into hers and said,
"Here—take your kid."

And just like that, I was back.
Standing in the same spot before the temple gates.
People were walking past me, staring, unaware of what
had just transpired.
I checked the time—
I had been standing there, motionless, for 45 minutes.

But I came back changed.

That day, I learned something most fear to accept:
Death is Gentle.
She is fierce, yes—but she is kind.
She is chaos, yes—but she is also a mother.
**And to those she protects, even fire becomes a path of
peace.**

21. The Ascent to Hemkund Sahib

There are some places you don't plan.
They call you.

Hemkund Sahib is one such place.
I didn't know it existed.
I had never even heard its name.
But somehow, I reached.

The original plan was to visit Badrinath and Kedarnath
in May 2022.
But just days before the journey, the path shifted.
The route changed to Badrinath and Hemkund Sahib—
one of the sacred sites of the Char Dham,
and the highest Gurudwara in the world, nestled at
14,200 feet.

The journey began from Govindghat.
From there, no vehicles take you further—only your feet
and your will.

Day 1:
A 10-kilometer hike to Ghangharia, a village embraced
by mist and mountains.

The path was steep, winding through thick forests and echoing silence.

But the real test had not yet begun.

Day 2:

The hike to Hemkund Sahib. Another 6 kilometers.

Only 6—but each step felt like lifting stone with your soul.

The air grew thinner, the slope steeper.

Mountains surrounded us like giants in prayer.

When just 2 kilometers remained, my body gave up.

I could no longer move.

It was almost 1 PM—

and the Gurudwara would close at 2 PM sharp due to the unpredictable weather.

I stood there, frozen in exhaustion, unsure if I would make it.

And in that moment of stillness,

I surrendered.

"You brought me this far... now You take me to You."

It was not a plea. It was a letting go.

And that's when I felt it—

For the first time in my life, I realised the mountains have energy.

Spirits.
Forces.
Invisible, yet present.
Something began to lift me—
not with strength, but with presence.

A sacred hand, unseen, guided me through those last
kilometers.
When I finally reached Hemkund Sahib at 1:40 PM, I
collapsed to my knees.
And then—
I saw Rushi and Andrea.

They ran toward me, and we embraced in tears.
All 3 of us cried.
We didn't speak. We didn't need to.
Something greater had moved all of us.

After offering my prayer in the Gurudwara, I stepped
outside—
to the edge of **Hemkund Lake**.

Surrounded by snow-draped peaks,
it shimmered like a mirror between worlds.

Still. Silent. Sacred.

I took 21 dips in the glacial water.
It was ice.
But it healed.
Each dip stripped something away—
fear, doubt, the fatigue of many lifetimes.

They say Guru Gobind Singh Ji meditated here in his
previous life.
And you can feel it—
The depth, the divinity.
The very air vibrates with that presence.

Hemkund Sahib is not just a Gurudwara.
It is a return to your essence.
To that moment when your body gives up,
but your spirit keeps walking.

9 789369 532315